COVER TO COVER

Lent
STUDY GUIDE

GW00371032

Living
Faith

Invitations from the cross

CWR

Krish Kandiah

© CWR 2017

Published 2017 by CWR, Waverley Abbey House, Waverley Lane, Farnham, Surrey GU9 8EP, UK. CWR is a Registered Charity – Number 294387 and a Limited Company registered in England – Registration Number 1990308. Reprinted 2018, 2019.

The right of Krish Kandiah to be identified as the author of this work has been asserted by him in accordance with the Copyright, Designs and Patents Act 1988, sections 77 and 78.

For a list of National Distributors. visit cwr.org.uk/distributors

Scripture references are taken from The Holy Bible, New International Version® Anglicised, NIV® Copyright © 1979, 1984, 2011 by Biblica, Inc.® Used by permission. All rights reserved worldwide.

Concept development, editing, design and production by CWR.

Every effort has been made to ensure that this book contains the correct permissions and references, but if anything has been inadvertently overlooked the Publisher will be pleased to make the necessary arrangements at the first opportunity. Please contact the Publisher directly.

Cover image: istockphoto.com/gabetorney, unsplash.com/codyleeaulidge, unsplash.com/Joshua Sortino.

Printed in the UK by Linney.

ISBN: 978-1-78259-691-2

Contents

Introduction

It can travel anywhere in time and space, and it looks much bigger on the inside (or smaller on the outside, depending on where you're standing). In 1963 it blended in perfectly as a British police box. But now, the intergalactic space cruiser stands out like a sore thumb, whether it's landed in contemporary London or in the Ancient Egyptian Sahara. It is strange, this foreign object that turns up in random places. And despite it being so alien – literally – nobody seems to bat an eyelid at the presence of The Doctor's TARDIS.

The cross of Christ is a similar anomaly. Worn as a fashion accessory, displayed in churches and schools and graveyards across the country, and gracing the lyrics of our worship songs and the walls of our art galleries – this ancient instrument of Roman execution has become one of the most recognisable symbols on the planet. And yet it often escapes people's notice. This Lent, I invite you to travel back in time to gaze intently at the cross of Jesus. Let's take time to explore the rich tapestry of meaning around the central and most defining moment in the history of the universe.

Like the TARDIS, the cross is an entry point to something much greater than its humble exterior would suggest. Something that seemed so commonplace and insignificant – such as a relatively unknown Jewish man dying at the hands of the Roman Empire – is, in fact, an invitation into a much larger reality. The cross opens up the depth of meaning in God's love, grace and compassion. It offers fresh faith for the doubter, new hope for the despondent, belonging for the lonely, and salvation for the lost. The cross is not just a celebration of death, but an invitation to life.

In this study guide, we'll adopt the ancient practice of remembering the final words of Jesus on the cross, as recorded in the Gospels, as the gateway in understanding the invitations that the cross offers. Each of these sayings from the cross can be seen as a unique invitation to connect

with God – what better way to prepare to celebrate Easter than an invitation from Jesus Himself to a deeper and living faith?

The last thing Jesus says as He dies on the cross are the definitive words: 'It is finished.' There are so many different ways in which those words are true. Jesus' own suffering is finished – He has identified with the pain of humanity to the utmost extreme. The old covenant sacrifice system is finished and done away with because the judgment of God is met with the sacrifice of His only Son. The captivity of humanity to sin is finished with the payment of the ransom necessary to liberate us. The Passover is finished as Jesus, the Lamb of God who takes away the sins of the world, fulfils all that God's rescue of His people from Egypt symbolised. The battle with evil is finished as Jesus, the conquering King, wins victory by dying in our place. Our exclusion from God's presence is finally over. Our pain and suffering is finished, as Jesus ushers in God's kingdom, where ultimately all tears will be forever washed away. Jesus was doing more than signaling the end of his life. He was declaring the completion of his mission and the beginning of something new for us.

After the decisive victory of D-Day in the Second World War, there was a period of time before the end of hostilities was declared on VE Day. Similarly, Jesus' earthly mission was completed at the cross, but we live in a period of time until its full implications will be realised. Jesus words, 'It is finished' are therefore an invitation to live in light of His victory. We know that the course of history has been set. When the world around us seems to be in disarray, darkness and despair, we can live confidently, knowing that Jesus has paid the price for the restoration of all things, and the reconciliation between heaven and earth.

There is a mystery to this invitation. Although we know that all evil has been defeated, we are yet to discover how all this will pan out. Jesus' declaration is therefore also an invitation to adventure, an invitation to trust, and an invitation to persevere. It is going to be an incredible journey, and as we work our way through these studies,

we will discover how all the other invitations of the cross light up our path.

So with the words 'It is finished' resounding in our ears, let's get started on the other six sayings of Jesus from the cross. May you discover another level of living faith as you hear and respond to Jesus' gracious words of invitation to you this Lent.

Invitation to forgiveness

'Father, forgive them'

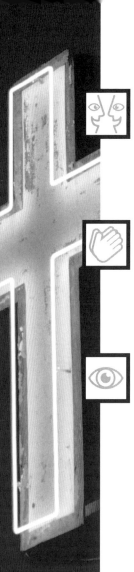

Warm Up

In pairs, think of some ordinary and extraordinary stories of forgiveness you have heard. They could be stories from your personal life, from fiction, or from the news. Alternatively, look up inspiring stories of forgiveness online. Why are these stories so powerful in today's world?

Opening Prayer

Father God, as we study this holy moment in human history where the Son of God laid down His life for us, please help us to hear His voice. Open our hearts to receive Your forgiveness and teach us how to pass on mercy to others. Challenge us, equip us, stir us and release us to walk the way of the cross today. Amen.

Eye Opener

In June 2016, UK Member of Parliament Jo Cox was murdered in broad daylight. The mother of two young children, she was less than a year in office but had invested her adult life campaigning on behalf of others – first with the charity Oxfam, and then in politics. The attack shocked the nation, but the response of her grieving husband was perhaps even more surprising:

> 'Today is the beginning of a new chapter in our lives.
> More difficult, more painful, less joyful, less full of love.
> I and Jo's friends and family are going to work every
> moment of our lives to love and nurture our kids and
> to fight against the hate that killed Jo… She would have
> wanted two things above all else to happen now, one that
> our precious children are bathed in love and two, that we
> all unite to fight against the hatred that killed her.'*

Brendan Cox's words of love, mercy and compassion – spoken just after the brutal killing of his wife, but also in the middle of a bitter and emotive political storm over Britain's place in Europe – modelled something powerful to the world. Cox claims no faith, or holds any spiritual convictions, but sets a powerful example to us all.

Setting the Scene

As Jesus was dying on the cross, there were words of hatred all around Him. Words of comfort or a revered silence would surely have been more welcome, but in the midst of severe physical pain and unimaginable spiritual distress, Jesus was tortured with mockery and verbal abuse from all sides.

We may know something of the difficulty of standing up for good when we are surrounded by evil. We may have had experience of fighting against our instinctive reaction to retaliate. But Jesus, surrounded by opposition, degradation and humiliation, responds by praying. He does not pray for Himself, but for His enemies – the very people who had put Him on that cross.

Jesus' suffering was of course unique, and yet Scripture tells us that because Jesus has suffered, He can empathise with us and our pain and struggles (Heb. 2:18). Perhaps you have suffered for standing up for what is right. Perhaps you spoke up at work against an unjust decision and were made to feel isolated for doing so. Perhaps you tried to lovingly tell a friend a truth they didn't want to hear and lost the friendship. Maybe, like many Christians around the world, you have faced some form of economic, social or even physical persecution. If you know something of the challenge of upholding good when you are surrounded by evil, you probably also know something of the temptation to retaliate, and the challenge of forgiveness.

As you read through these two Bible passages, ask the Holy Spirit to make them alive, to challenge, provoke and inspire you to hear Jesus' invitation to forgiveness.

Bible Readings

Luke 23:32–38
'Two other men, both criminals, were also led out
with him to be executed. When they came to the place
called the Skull, they crucified him there, along with
the criminals – one on his right, the other on his left.
Jesus said, "Father, forgive them, for they do not know
what they are doing." And they divided up his clothes by
casting lots. The people stood watching, and the rulers
even sneered at him. They said, "He saved others; let him
save himself if he is God's Messiah, the Chosen One." The
soldiers also came up and mocked him. They offered him
wine vinegar and said, "If you are the king of the Jews,
save yourself." There was a written notice above him,
which read: 'THIS IS THE KING OF THE JEWS.'

Ephesians 4:29–32
'Do not let any unwholesome talk come out of your
mouths, but only what is helpful for building others
up according to their needs, that it may benefit those
who listen. And do not grieve the Holy Spirit of God,
with whom you were sealed for the day of redemption.
Get rid of all bitterness, rage and anger, brawling and
slander, along with every form of malice. Be kind and
compassionate to one another, forgiving each other, just
as in Christ God forgave you.'

Session Focus

The scene of Jesus' death was brutal. Firstly, there was an
unsympathetic crowd gathered to watch Him die. It is possible
that some of those present were the same people who just
a week earlier had laid down their coats and waved palm
branches for Him, chanting, 'Hosanna' as He entered Jerusalem
on a donkey. Perhaps they had been there when Pilate offered
the people a choice between the carpenter's son from Nazareth,
or Jerusalem's most-wanted villain, Barabbas, and they had

pointed at Jesus and chanted, 'Crucify him!' In just a week their applause had turned to disappointment, and then to anger. He was not the Messiah they expected.

Secondly, Jesus faced opposition from the religious rulers, who were not there to administer the last rites or to offer Him consolation, but to ridicule Him for not being the Saviour they expected: 'He saved others: let him save himself.' Jesus' words of warning to this group of people, whom He perhaps expected to have known better, were ignored.

Thirdly, the Roman Procurator Pontius Pilate used this execution to mock both Jesus and the Jews by affixing a sign to the cross that acted like a punchline under a satirical cartoon. Pilate's comment on the agony of Jesus was no less dismissive: 'THIS IS THE KING OF THE JEWS.' Crucifixion was an obscene public address system employed by Rome to strike fear into its subjects. It was, as Nolland writes, 'a form of execution by torture; it was about as cruel and barbaric as any deterrent dreamed up by humankind. The idea was to prolong the agony of death for all to see and be warned.'** Pilate wanted the world to know that this 'criminal', bleeding, suffering and dying, could never live up to the title and the people's expectations of a king.

Fourthly, the Roman soldiers mocked Jesus with no restraint whatsoever. A man nailed to a cross was a very potent visual aid of the futility of challenging the might of Imperial Rome. And as if the humiliation of being stripped naked and crucified at the town's rubbish dump wasn't degrading enough, the soldiers verbally abused Jesus, hurling their insults at Him: 'If you are the king of the Jews, save yourself.' With no army and no weapons, Jesus was not the kind of King they expected. Their offer of wine vinegar was a gesture of scorn and hostility – cheap wine for a cheap king.

After all that hate, Jesus' response is astonishing. He asks God to forgive. For whom is Jesus pleading forgiveness? His executioners, who were soldiers just doing their jobs? The crowds, who, when they called for Jesus' death, didn't realise what they were asking for? Or the Jewish nation, for rejecting the Messiah? Or the whole of humankind represented by the

Jewish people and the Romans; Jews and Gentiles together being forgiven? It is difficult to decipher from the Gospel account. But there does not seem to be a limit on Jesus' request to His Father for forgiveness. He does not appear to be restricting His forgiveness to the Romans or the Jews, to the religious leaders or the pagan soldiers. Jesus' request that God forgive seems to be aimed at all those who are mocking, wounding, insulting, murdering and opposing Him. Perhaps it is even extended to us, whose acts of sin and betrayal were part of the reason Jesus hung dying that day.

There is a stark contrast here. On one hand, there are those who see Jesus, broken and bruised, and then decide to further wound Him by spitting their insults at Him. On the other hand, we see Jesus, looking down from the cross at His enemies gloating and taunting Him, and yet He speaks grace and compassion.

I find Jesus' actions and words deeply challenging to me in how I treat the people in my life. Jesus invites us to both receive forgiveness from Him, and to offer forgiveness to others. Paul reminds us of the link in Ephesians 4:32. And in Brendon Cox's response to his wife's brutal and public murder, we see an example of what it means today to fight brutality with forgiveness, division with unity, and hatred with love. Like him, we are called to follow Jesus' example of showing grace under fire; mercy in the face of evil.

Discussion Starters

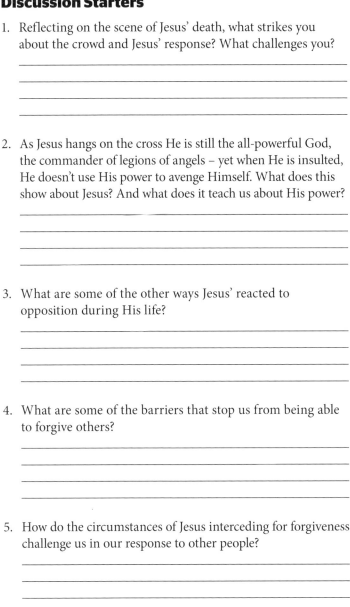

1. Reflecting on the scene of Jesus' death, what strikes you about the crowd and Jesus' response? What challenges you?

_____

_____

_____

_____

2. As Jesus hangs on the cross He is still the all-powerful God, the commander of legions of angels – yet when He is insulted, He doesn't use His power to avenge Himself. What does this show about Jesus? And what does it teach us about His power?

_____

_____

_____

_____

3. What are some of the other ways Jesus' reacted to opposition during His life?

_____

_____

_____

_____

4. What are some of the barriers that stop us from being able to forgive others?

_____

_____

_____

_____

5. How do the circumstances of Jesus interceding for forgiveness challenge us in our response to other people?

_____

_____

_____

_____

6. When was the last time you had to ask for forgiveness from someone? How did it feel to ask? Was forgiveness given to you? How did you feel after?

_____

_____

_____

_____

7. How might you advise a Christian friend who says they are struggling to forgive someone?

_____

_____

_____

_____

_____

8. Read Ephesians 4:29–31. How would you most like to develop your 'Christlikeness'?

_____

_____

_____

_____

Final Thoughts

Jesus' forgiveness at extreme personal cost is a powerful invitation to all of us. Too often we live with the guilt and shame of our sin that Jesus has paid to remove. Come to Jesus who interceded on your behalf centuries before you ever did anything wrong. He wants you to know God's liberating forgiveness.

Jesus' forgiveness under extreme pressure challenges us to look at some of the hurts we may still carry from the past and to apply the transforming grace of forgiveness to these broken relationships. Similarly, whether there are others that we need to seek forgiveness from.

Forgiveness is powerful, but it is incredibly costly. It cost Jesus' life to make our forgiveness possible. We should not expect it to be simple for us to forgive others.

Jesus' forgiveness for people headed for an eternity without God is also an effective example for us. Let us advocate like Him on behalf of friends and strangers to be convicted by the Holy Spirit and discover God's forgiveness in their lives.

We have touched on some personal and challenging issues this week. As we close in prayer, pray for those in situations where it is hard to offer or receive forgiveness.

Closing Prayer

Our Father in heaven,
hallowed be Your name,
Your kingdom come,
Your will be done,
on earth as in heaven.
Give us today our daily bread.
Forgive us our sins
as we forgive those who sin against us.
Lead us not into temptation
but deliver us from evil.
For the kingdom, the power,
and the glory are Yours
now and forever.
Amen.

▶❚❚ Further Reflection

Forgiveness is a rich and powerful theme in the Bible. You can explore it further by reading the story of Joseph, which starts in Genesis 37. The following books are also very helpful on this issue:

Johann Christoph Arnold, *Why Forgive?* (Robertsbridge: Plough Publishing, 2010)

Ron Kallmier and Sheila Jacobs, *Insight into Forgiveness* (Farnham; CWR, 2008)

Miroslav Volf, *Free of Charge: Giving and Forgiving in a Culture Stripped of Grace* (Grand Rapids, MI, USA: Zondervan, 2006)

*BBC News, 16 June 2016: www.bbc.co.uk/news (Accessed 1 June 2017)

**J. Nolland (1998), 'Luke' (Vol. 35C), *Word Biblical Commentary on the New Testament* (Dallas, TX, USA: Word, 1998), p1148

Invitation to service

'I am thirsty'

Warm Up

Offer a blind tasting session of various non-alcoholic drinks and see if people can identify them. Include vinegar or wine vinegar. Other options could include cold tea, fruit juices, dilute cordials, flavoured waters or milks, flat cola etc. Discuss the reactions.

Opening Prayer

'As the deer pants for streams of water, so my soul pants for you, my God. My soul thirsts for God, for the living God' (Psa. 42:1–2). Lord, we come to You thirsty today – thirsty for Your Word, for Your presence, for Your love, for Your peace and for Your wisdom. Thank You for all of Your gifts of provision to us. Amen.

Eye Opener

I was 16 years old when Russian customs officers found illegal Bibles in my suitcase. I was terrified! But instead of arresting me, they asked if I could spare a copy for them to keep!

That mission trip, I discovered that I was not bringing God to Russians as expected – God was already there. In one home, a man cooked for us Russian pancakes and caviar. What I assumed to be his standard evening meal was actually a treat he had been saving for years for a special occasion with honoured guests. I have never forgotten his example of humility and hospitality.

Setting the Scene

Jesus frequently fed the hungry. We think of the boy who offered his meagre picnic of fish and bread, and how Jesus turned it into lunch for thousands. We remember how Jesus helped weary fishermen make a record catch, and how, after His resurrection, He prepared a breakfast barbecue on the beach for His astonished disciples.

But Jesus was more often a guest than a host, and was on the receiving end of hospitality right from birth. Arriving in Bethlehem, Mary and Joseph had to rely on the kindness of a busy innkeeper for shelter. Later as an adult, Jesus was a guest in the homes of the tax collector Zacchaeus and the judgmental Pharisees. In fact, Jesus received hospitality from all the 'wrong' sort of people and was often criticised for it. But He was not ashamed. Despite protests from onlookers, He received the welcome given Him by Mary Magdalene, who poured pure nard (an expensive perfume) on His feet. He was not reluctant to ask a woman by a well in Samaria for a drink. Now, in the second of Jesus' words from the cross, Jesus again asks for a drink, this time from His enemies. As we look closer at Jesus inviting the most unlikely people to serve Him, we discover a powerful challenge for how we can respond to the needs of others.

Bible Readings

John 19:28–30

'Later, knowing that everything had now been finished, and so that Scripture would be fulfilled, Jesus said, "I am thirsty." A jar of wine vinegar was there, so they soaked a sponge in it, put the sponge on a stalk of the hyssop plant, and lifted it to Jesus' lips. When he had received the drink, Jesus said, "It is finished." With that, he bowed his head and gave up his spirit.'

Matthew 25:34–40

'Then the King will say to those on his right, "Come, you who are blessed by my Father; take your inheritance, the kingdom prepared for you since the creation of the world. For I was hungry and you gave me something to eat, I was thirsty and you gave me something to drink, I was a stranger and you invited me in, I needed clothes and you clothed me, I was ill and you looked after me, I was in prison and you came to visit me." Then the

righteous will answer him, "Lord, when did we see you hungry and feed you, or thirsty and give you something to drink? When did we see you a stranger and invite you in, or needing clothes and clothe you? When did we see you ill or in prison and go to visit you?" The King will reply, "Truly I tell you, whatever you did for one of the least of these brothers and sisters of mine, you did for me.'"

Session Focus

When Jesus lets us know from the cross that He is thirsty, we get a glimpse of His genuine humanity. Just like us, Jesus' body experienced hunger, thirst and pain. Jesus was not God pretending to be human. Jesus as God in human flesh experienced all the same difficulties and weaknesses that we have. When we pray to Him, we can be sure that he empathises with us: He understands our pain, our tiredness, our loneliness and our isolation.

There is something beautiful and tragic about the fact that Jesus is thirsty on the cross. The poet Thomas Pollock writes eloquently about Jesus' humanity in these words:

Jesus, in Thy thirst and pain,
While Thy wounds Thy life-blood drain,
Thirsting more our love to gain:
Hear us, holy Jesus.

Thirst for us in mercy still,
Satisfy Thy loving will:
All Thy holy work fulfil.
Hear us, holy Jesus.

May we thirst Thy love to know;
Lead us in our sin and woe
Where the healing waters flow:
Hear us, holy Jesus.

(Thomas B. Pollock, 1836–1896)

But there is mystery here. The one who offered others the water of life so that we would never be thirsty again, is thirsty. The one who is described in 1 Corinthians 10 as the 'rock' from which God's people had their thirst quenched, is thirsty. The one who promised to satisfy those who thirst for righteousness, is thirsty. The omnipotent one who walked on water, calmed the waters of the storm, and turned water into wine, is thirsty.

But even more profoundly, the one who created water, and separated the waters above from the waters below at the beginning of time, is thirsty. The one who raised others from the dead, and is now dying Himself, asks someone to bring Him a drink.

When Jesus brings the wine to the party it is the best wine anyone has ever tasted, but when Jesus is thirsty, humanity brings Him the cheap stuff. The one who has healed thousands, fed thousands, is not given anything more than a mouthful of wine lifted up on a hyssop stalk – a plant known for its healing qualities. It was His last request, but the response was an insult: a spongeful of bitterness raised on a stick of irony.

As Jesus slowly suffocates on the cross, His body bruised and battered, His back stinging from the whipping He's received, we offer Him the least, the leftovers, the cheap stuff.

When I was a child I used to imagine myself finding a time machine, maybe hitching a lift with the Doctor in the TARDIS, and going back in time to rescue Jesus from the cross. I was too young in my faith to understand that Jesus could easily have rescued Himself from the cross. He is the omnipotent God! He has command of legions of angels! He certainly did not need the help of a twentieth-century, nine-year-old Asian boy to get Him out of the hands of the Romans. Later I understood that, but I nevertheless would commandeer the TARDIS in a moment, if I thought I could bring Jesus some relief on the cross. And I would not bring cheap alcohol, the kind of stuff that teenagers might buy to get drunk on in a supermarket car park. I would want to find something worthy of the King of kings – the best that I could afford.

'I am thirsty,' says Jesus. What would you have brought the Son of God who was dying there on the cross to secure your eternal destiny? The reality is that we do not need a TARDIS

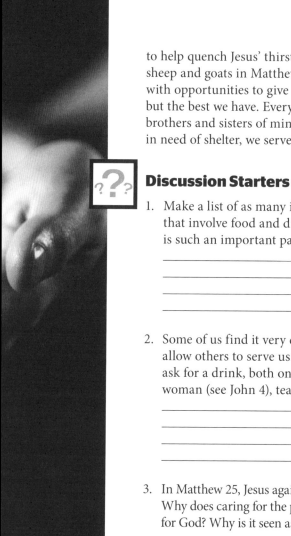

to help quench Jesus' thirst. According to the parable of the sheep and goats in Matthew 25, Jesus clearly provides us with opportunities to give – not the leftovers, the cheap stuff, but the best we have. Every time we serve 'the least of these brothers and sisters of mine' who is hungry, thirsty, naked or in need of shelter, we serve Jesus.

Discussion Starters

1. Make a list of as many incidents in Jesus' life as you can that involve food and drink. Why do you think hospitality is such an important part of Jesus' ministry?

_____

_____

_____

_____

2. Some of us find it very difficult to admit our needs and allow others to serve us. What does Jesus' willingness to ask for a drink, both on the cross and from the Samaritan woman (see John 4), teach us?

_____

_____

_____

_____

3. In Matthew 25, Jesus again describes Himself as being thirsty. Why does caring for the poor and needy demonstrate our love for God? Why is it seen as the test of genuine faith?

_____

_____

_____

_____

4. How would you respond if someone said: 'Evangelism is the main priority of the Church. Providing for those in need is less important.' Or, 'Providing for those in need is my evangelism. Words tend to complicate things.'

_____

_____

_____

_____

5. Jesus refers to 'the least of these brothers and sisters of mine'. What evidence is there in the Bible that it's not just believers to whom we should offer hospitality?

_____

_____

_____

_____

6. Where are the opportunities in your family, church, and community to serve Jesus by serving those in need?

_____

_____

_____

_____

7. Hebrews 13:2 says: 'Do not forget to show hospitality to strangers, for by so doing some people have shown hospitality to angels without knowing it.' How has serving others impacted your own spiritual life?

_____

_____

_____

_____

8. How can our own feeling of thirst help remind us of the most important themes in Scripture?

_____

_____

_____

_____

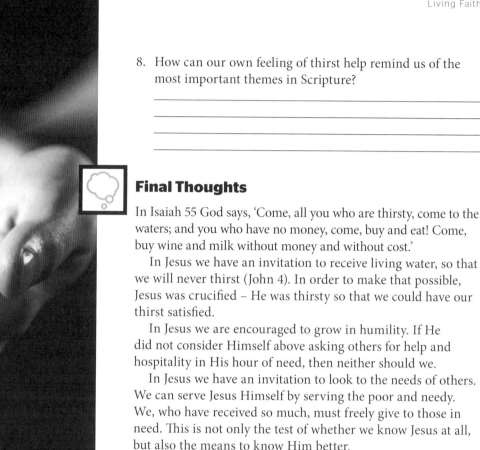

Final Thoughts

In Isaiah 55 God says, 'Come, all you who are thirsty, come to the waters; and you who have no money, come, buy and eat! Come, buy wine and milk without money and without cost.'

In Jesus we have an invitation to receive living water, so that we will never thirst (John 4). In order to make that possible, Jesus was crucified – He was thirsty so that we could have our thirst satisfied.

In Jesus we are encouraged to grow in humility. If He did not consider Himself above asking others for help and hospitality in His hour of need, then neither should we.

In Jesus we have an invitation to look to the needs of others. We can serve Jesus Himself by serving the poor and needy. We, who have received so much, must freely give to those in need. This is not only the test of whether we know Jesus at all, but also the means to know Him better.

Closing Prayer

Father God, God of the poor, the thirsty, the hungry, the naked and the lonely, we are grateful for all that You have given to us through Jesus. By Your Spirit, inspire us to serve those in need as if we are serving Christ Himself. Give us eyes to see and hands that arc quick to help. Amen.

Further Reflection

You could further meditate on this theme by reading Isaiah 58. The following books also explore the topic:

Krish Kandiah, *God Is Stranger: What happens when God turns up?* (London: Hodder & Stoughton, 2017)

Steve Corbett and Brian Fikkert, *When Helping Hurts* (Chicago, IL, USA: Moody Publishers, 2014)

Invitation to hope

'Today you will be with me in paradise'

Warm Up

What would you describe as a 'life-changing' experience? How might such experiences change the way people live, and can negative experiences ever impact lives in a positive way? Discuss these questions as a group.

Opening Prayer

Our Father God, who will judge the living and the dead, we thank You for the life You have given to us. We ask for Your help as we reflect on Your invitation to hope. By Your Spirit would You guide our study and help us to gain fresh hope for today, for tomorrow and for all eternity. Amen.

Eye Opener

Sometimes it takes a brush with death to really understand life. After a friend of mine had emergency heart surgery, he developed a very different outlook. What he used to take for granted, he is now determined to appreciate and use well. But it doesn't have to be a personal near-death experience that changes us. Sometimes it is the mortality of others. For so many people, the atrocities of 9/11 were a turning point in their lives. The death of Jesus, brutal and shocking though that was, offers a turning point too – an invitation to a new way of life.

Setting the Scene

It is in the exchange of words between Jesus and the other criminal dying beside Him that we are given an insight into the welcome God is offering to us amid the trauma and tragedy of crucifixion. Can you imagine how painful speaking even a single word would have been for any of those men, slowly suffocating to death while being nailed to a cross? Trying to get a word out would have been excruciating, as slow asphyxiation through exhaustion was the ultimate cause of death behind crucifixion. Yet Jesus chooses to use some of His last painful breaths to speak words of comfort and compassion to a stranger.

At the cross of Christ is a story of incredible grace. At the heart of atonement is divine hospitality, where God invites the undeserving and unexpected to come home with Him. This is a very precious part of the Bible to me, as I have seen God use it to help many people come to faith. It is beautiful that just as Jesus is dying to give humans the opportunity of forgiveness, He takes time to help the one right next to Him. Many would have rejected this man as a lost cause, as a worthless criminal, as a nobody – but Jesus singles him out, offering hope not only to him, but to so many others throughout the centuries.

Bible Readings

Luke 23:39–43

'One of the criminals who hung there hurled insults at him: "Aren't you the Messiah? Save yourself and us!" But the other criminal rebuked him. "Don't you fear God," he said, "since you are under the same sentence? We are punished justly, for we are getting what our deeds deserve. But this man has done nothing wrong." Then he said, "Jesus, remember me when you come into your kingdom." Jesus answered him, "Truly I tell you, today you will be with me in paradise."'

2 Corinthians 1:3–7

'Praise be to the God and Father of our Lord Jesus Christ, the Father of compassion and the God of all comfort, who comforts us in all our troubles, so that we can comfort those in any trouble with the comfort we ourselves receive from God. For just as we share abundantly in the sufferings of Christ, so also our comfort abounds through Christ. If we are distressed, it is for your comfort and salvation; if we are comforted, it is for your comfort, which produces in you patient endurance of the same sufferings we suffer. And our hope for you is firm, because we know that just as you share in our sufferings, so also you share in our comfort.'

Session Focus

When I was studying chemistry at university, I was mentored by a brilliant Bible teacher and evangelist. He helped me to grow in my love for God, and gave me a passion for Scripture and for helping other people to encounter God in its pages. I don't think I would be writing a Bible study guide today if it hadn't been for that mentoring relationship.

A few years ago, he contracted cancer and was in hospital for a last-ditch chemotherapy treatment. The doctors had told him it was unlikely to have an effect, but they recommended it nonetheless. He spent his evenings in the cancer ward visiting his fellow patients. Some of them were too weak to move, so he would sit next to them on the bed listening and talking with them. Some asked him if he was afraid to die, and he took the opportunity to explain about his hope in Jesus. This man had spent his adult life as a Bible teacher and evangelist; he had travelled the world explaining the gospel and had an immeasurable impact on me as a student, helping me to come to grips with my faith amid all the scepticism I found at university. But as a dying man speaking to other dying men, his witness to the Christian faith took on a new level of authority and contagion. In a pretty hopeless situation, his hope shone bright.

As Jesus hung on the cross, three dying men got into conversation. One man, a self-confessed criminal, joined in with the sneers of the crowds. But the other, also a criminal, interjected: 'Don't you fear God... since you are under the same sentence? We are punished justly, for we are getting what our deeds deserve. But this man has done nothing wrong.' In the middle of this maelstrom of malevolence, one voice stood out to offer an alternative view of the situation. This criminal's last words show that he saw what everyone else seemed to miss. He alone identified three crucial things about Jesus.

First, he recognised Jesus' solidarity with them: all three men were in the same boat, facing the same fate. They were all about to suffer death at the hands of a brutal Roman regime. Secondly, he perceived Jesus' sanctity: the criminal noticed a fundamental difference between himself and Jesus. While everyone else saw a would-be 'king', an impotent 'saviour' and a disappointing and blaspheming 'messiah', this criminal alone saw his own guilt and Jesus' innocence of all charges.

Finally, the criminal recognised Jesus' sovereignty. The criminal saw in Jesus a king – despite the fact that Jesus was naked, dying on a cross, no hint of pomp or splendour about Him. Despite the mocking sign nailed to the cross and the ironic crown of thorns rammed on His head, the criminal saw the truth about Jesus. He somehow knew that Jesus would enter His own kingdom on His death.

Looking back on this incident now, with the benefit of 2,000 years of theological reflection on the death of Christ, it is hard to grasp the profound level of understanding this criminal demonstrates about the events he was caught up in. Apart from Jesus Himself, it seems that no one at all had understood that the crucifixion was not a terrible miscarriage of justice, but was the very means by which Jesus was going to be crowned King. Jesus endorses His neighbour's take on events, graciously responding with the assurance that has become treasured as the third of seven sayings of Jesus from the cross: 'Today you will be with me in paradise.'

Jesus wants this self-confessed criminal, guilty of a capital crime, to be in no doubt that He will shortly be receiving the ultimate VIP welcome, personally accompanied by the King of heaven Himself. He solemnly promises the thief the two key things he needs to know – he will be with Jesus, and he will be in paradise. What an invitation to hope for a man in desperate need. Just like my mentor walking that cancer ward, Jesus offers true hope as a dying man to dying men.

? Discussion Starters

1. What strikes you as strange about the conversation between the three dying men?

   _____

   _____

   _____

   _____

2. How do you think Jesus' promise to the thief on the cross that, 'Today you will be with me in paradise' made him feel?

   _____

   _____

   _____

   _____

3. How confident do you feel that, if you were to die, you too would be with Jesus in paradise?

   _____

   _____

   _____

   _____

4. What would help you to have assurance of the hope that Jesus promises? Look at the 2 Corinthians passage for encouragement.

   _____

   _____

   _____

   _____

5. Jesus invites us to new hope. He also models to us inviting others into new hope. When was the last time you talked to someone about faith? How did it go?

   _____

   _____

   _____

   _____

6. What do you find most difficult about sharing your hope, or sharing your faith? How can this study encourage you?

_____

_____

_____

_____

7. Read the 2 Corinthians passage again. There is a connection made between suffering and comfort, salvation and hope. How can our understanding of suffering – either our own or others' – give us a fresh vision for sharing our faith?

_____

_____

_____

_____

8. Think of people who really need hope in their lives right now. How can we invite them to experience the hope that we have?

_____

_____

_____

_____

Final Thoughts

I have heard many people talk about how difficult it is to witness about Jesus in our day and age – there is so much to lose, so many risks and dangers. Western culture is changing, church going is declining, biblical and faith literacy seems to be diminishing. As a result of these trends, the Church has lost a degree of confidence, and we are increasingly nervous to speak up about our faith and to be identified with Jesus.

But the invitation to hope that Jesus issues from the cross to a dying criminal should challenge us. We follow a master who was killed for (and while) living and preaching the gospel. Thanks to Jesus, we have been given a hope not only for life but, even more miraculously, for life beyond death. This is a

precious gift to which nothing else on earth can compare. Even in His dying breath, Jesus is inviting others to life and hope, joy and eternity with Him. Will we, who claim to follow in Jesus' footsteps, do the same? Will we take every opportunity to invite the world to this hope too, no matter what the cost?

Closing Prayer

Dear loving heavenly Father, we thank You for the hope of resurrection we have through Jesus' death. We thank You for the hope of life we have through Jesus' sacrifice. We thank You for the hope of paradise we have through Jesus' agony. Help us to trust Christ's promise, whatever our feelings. Help us to share the hope we have, whatever the cost. Amen.

Further Reflection

1 Corinthians 15 explores the difference that having a hope of life beyond death should make to our lives. These books may be helpful too:

J. I. Packer, *Finishing Our Course With Joy* (Downers Grove, IL, USA: IVP, 2014)

J. Stott, *The Cross of Christ* (Leicester: IVP, 1995)

Invitation to adoption

'Here is your son... Here is your mother'

Warm Up

How many fostered or adopted children can you name in film and literature? James Bond, Jane Eyre, Luke Skywalker, Harry Potter, Alex Rider, Mary Lennox... Do they have anything in common in their attitudes towards life and other people?

Opening Prayer

Lord God, thank You for the families you have placed us in, and for those who love, support, encourage and care for us. Thank You for Your loving care too, Father, and for adopting us as Your children. Despite the mess we were in, You welcomed us into Your family. Please give us open hearts to all You have to say to us today. Amen.

Eye Opener

One of the hardest things we have to do as foster carers, is say goodbye to children we have welcomed into our family and loved as our own. It is a unique grief. A lingering heartache. Fingerprints on walls and small socks at the bottom of the washing basket can bring tears to our eyes for months afterwards. Photographs can make us cry even years later. But handing a child over to adopters is also one of the most amazing privileges of being a foster carer. Seeing a parent meet a longed-for child, and a child meet a much-needed forever parent is a precious moment indeed.

Setting the Scene

Jesus, the Son of God who has done nothing wrong, is dying for the sins of the world. But in the midst of unimaginable pain and agony while hanging on the cross, He still makes time to sort out His family arrangements. There has been a strange tension in the Gospels regarding Jesus and family. First, Jesus calls believers to be willing to leave their families and follow Him, recognising that the call to discipleship may divide families. But Jesus also challenges those who would abdicate family responsibilities, by declaring money they would have given to their families, as 'Corban' or money committed to God's work (see Mark 7:11). Even with Jesus' own family there is tension when His mother and brothers turn up to a venue where He is speaking, ask for Him at the door and Jesus doesn't instantly go to them. Instead He identifies the disciples as His family, pointing to them and saying, 'Whoever does the will of my Father in heaven is my brother and sister and mother' (Matt. 12:47–50). Yet here we are at the foot of the cross, and we witness something quite beautiful in how Jesus cares for both His mother and His disciple.

Bible Readings

John 19:25–27
'Near the cross of Jesus stood his mother, his mother's sister, Mary the wife of Clopas, and Mary Magdalene. When Jesus saw his mother there, and the disciple whom he loved standing near by, he said to her, "Woman, here is your son," and to the disciple, "Here is your mother" From that time on, this disciple took her into his home.'

James 1:22–27
'Do not merely listen to the word, and so deceive yourselves. Do what it says. Anyone who listens to the word but does not do what it says is like someone who looks at his face in a mirror and, after looking at himself, goes away and immediately forgets what he looks like. But whoever looks intently into the perfect law that gives freedom and continues in it – not forgetting what they have heard but doing it – they will be blessed in what they do. Those who consider themselves religious and yet do not keep a tight rein on their tongues deceive themselves, and their religion is worthless. Religion that God our Father accepts as pure and faultless is this: to look after orphans and widows in their distress and to keep oneself from being polluted by the world.'

Session Focus

As Jesus hangs on the cross, John records His fourth saying. Jesus turns to His mother Mary and His friend John, and mandates both of them to care for one another like a son and a mother. As if dying for the sins of the world and securing our eternal home wasn't a big enough task, even as He dies, Jesus secures temporal homes for those closest to Him.

The highly respected New Testament scholar D.A. Carson recognises in Jesus' formal words the echo of a legal adoption formula, and John himself tells us that, 'From that time on, this disciple took her into his home.' John adopted Mary as his own mother, to care for her needs and to console her in this time of great personal loss. What happened to Jesus' brothers, the natural-born sons that Joseph and Mary had together, is uncertain. Perhaps they were still estranged from Jesus, or perhaps they were just not in Jerusalem at the time. Nevertheless, in this simple act we see Jesus enabling people to be reconciled both to God and to one another.

In the Psalms we are told that 'God sets the lonely in families' (Psa. 68:6). This is an interesting turn of phrase, as we are all born into families of some kind. But the context of this psalm describes it is those who have lost their natural families – the widow and the orphan – that God takes special care of: 'A father to the fatherless, a defender of widows, is God in his holy dwelling' (v6). So here we see Jesus doing that, in a very practical way, for His birth mother. She is a widow losing her son, and so Jesus is making sure Mary is set in a family.

Sometimes we can over-spiritualise the Christian faith – we can make it all about *our* relationship with God, as if other people are just an optional extra. We close our eyes in worship, take silent retreats and do our personal devotions. But for Jesus, there is no such separation. Worshipping God and including others go hand in hand. Worship might be a comfortable musical interlude in our lives – we sing some soft rock songs, or four-part harmonic hymns, or some gospel tunes or simple familiar choruses – but there is no musical soundtrack to the death of Jesus. At the holiest moment in human history, there is not a lot of singing going on. But there is an adoption – practical care for the widow and the orphan.

I have heard people explain to me that their lives are too busy to care for the vulnerable, or too focused – they have other 'ministry priorities'. Even church pastors have said this to me. Yet somehow, while He was dying for the sins of the world (which I would have thought would have been a very acceptable 'ministry priority'), Jesus had enough time to instigate an adoption to make sure a widow was cared for.

I find it very challenging that Jesus, who had every excuse for caring for His own needs as He took on the sins of the world, even in this moment of extreme crisis was looking out for the needs of others. Whether it was the repentant criminal dying next to Him, or His widowed and grieving mother, or His distraught disciple – He made sure He did all He could for them.

As we see Jesus in action, we learn again that we show our love for God by loving our neighbour. We are most like Jesus when we show concern for the poor, vulnerable and isolated. We demonstrate the grace of God by the way we care for those without families, without protection or without a voice. As James said: 'Religion that God our Father accepts as pure and faultless is this: to look after orphans and widows in their distress and to keep oneself from being polluted by the world' (James 1:27).

Discussion Starters

1. Why does Jesus make this formal pronouncement about His mother and His friend John? What does it say about His understanding of His role as God's Son, and as a human son?

   _____

   _____

   _____

   _____

2. How does this invitation to John and Mary illustrate the work of the cross? How does the picture of adoption help you to understand and appreciate your salvation?

   _____

   _____

   _____

   _____

3. As part of an earthly family, what positive attitudes does Jesus model here? How can we incorporate these into our own family lives?

   _____

   _____

   _____

   _____

4. Why do you think James 1:27 makes caring for widows and orphans the litmus test of genuine spiritual worship and the right attitude to Scripture?

   _____

   _____

   _____

   _____

5. Why were widows and orphans particularly vulnerable in the ancient world? Who are the equivalent people in our society today who are most vulnerable?

_____

_____

_____

_____

6. What different attitudes towards foster care and adoption have you come across? If you know a family that has fostered or adopted, what has their experience been like?

_____

_____

_____

_____

7. There are 5,000 children in the UK who are waiting to be welcomed into a permanent family. What do you think the Church's role could be in responding to this need?

_____

_____

_____

_____

8. How can we, as a Church, extend an invitation to others to join our spiritual family, and also help find physical homes for those who need one?

_____

_____

_____

_____

Final Thoughts

I hadn't realised how important adoption is to our relationship with God until after we had adopted our fourth child. It was in the experience of welcoming someone else's child into our family, and promising and pledging to love her as our own flesh and blood, that I came to understand the beauty of the Bible's doctrine of adoption. We did not need another child – we already had three. She was never going to be the perfect child to make us look good – she came broken and scarred. And yet we loved her just the same and just as much as we loved our other children. Not only that, but in blessing her we too were blessed beyond what we could ever have imagined.

How much more amazing is God's welcome to us as broken children in need of His love and care. The more I reflect on this, the more I realise the powerful visual aid of God's adopting grace in our lives that comes through our care for vulnerable children.

Closing Prayer

Praise be to the God and Father of our Lord Jesus Christ. For He chose us in Him before the creation of the world to be holy and blameless in His sight. In love, He predestined us for adoption through Jesus, to the praise of His glorious grace, which He has freely given us in the one He loves. Amen. (Based on Eph. 1:3–6.)

Further Reflection

To meditate more on the idea of adoption in Scripture, read Romans 8 and notice how our adoption is linked to the restoration of all things.

Some more suggested reading:

Krish and Miriam Kandiah, *Home for Good: Making a difference for vulnerable children* (London: Hodder & Stoughton, 2013)

Dan Cruver (Ed.), *Reclaiming Adoption: Missional Living through the Rediscovery of Abba Father* (Hudson, OH, USA: Cruciform Press, 2011)

.

Invitation to empathy

'My God, why have you forsaken me?'

Warm Up

If you're comfortable doing so, split into pairs. Decide who will be speaker and who will be listener. The speaker is to talk about something that happened today, and how they felt about it. The listener is to ask questions to help them understand the other person's feelings. After five minutes, the listener should reflect back to the speaker what they heard and understood. The speaker should then say how well they think the listener understood them.

Opening Prayer

Dear all-knowing God, thank You that You know us so completely. You know the words we are going to say before we even open our mouths. You know where we have been, what we have done, and all the days marked before us. You know each and every hair on our head. Thank You that You understand us. Amen.

Eye Opener

Theoretically, we know that God knows everything. But experientially, God can often feel very far from us. We may pour out prayers to Him but it feels like no one is listening; as if God doesn't understand, and isn't fulfilling His promises to us. There seems to be a gap between what we know to be true, and how we experience things in reality. This can make it difficult to trust, to pray, to worship, to serve, to hope and to care. As Christians, this may be something we are unwilling to admit but it's a common struggle.

Setting the Scene

Jesus knew what was ahead of Him on the cross. He understood God's will for His life and He knew the extent of the need around Him in the world. He understood the Old Testament theme of sacrifice and was familiar with the prophecies about the details of the cross. He knew from the beginning of time that it was always part of the plan that He would carry the sins of the world. This was something He predicted numerous times in His own teaching, along with the resurrection.

For example, in Mark 8:31, Jesus speaks plainly about His death: 'He then began to teach them that the Son of Man must suffer many things and be rejected by the elders, the chief priests and the teachers of the law, and that he must be killed and after three days rise again.' This is not a one-off occasion – three times He repeats this prediction. Yet on the cross, before Jesus cries out in victory, 'It is finished', He utters a cry of desolation: 'My God, my God, why have you forsaken me?' As we listen to the Bible being read to us today, let's try to imagine and think about what Jesus is experiencing and why He is using this powerfully evocative language.

Bible Readings

Mark 15:33–36
'At noon, darkness came over the whole land until three in the afternoon. And at three in the afternoon Jesus cried out in a loud voice, *"Eloi, Eloi, lama sabachthani?"* (which means "My God, my God, why have you forsaken me?"). When some of those standing near heard this, they said, "Listen, he's calling Elijah." Someone ran, filled a sponge with wine vinegar, put it on a staff, and offered it to Jesus to drink. "Now leave him alone. Let's see if Elijah comes to take him down," he said.'

Psalm 22:1–15
'My God, my God, why have you forsaken me?
Why are you so far from saving me,
so far from my cries of anguish?
My God, I cry out by day, but you do not answer,
by night, but I find no rest.
Yet you are enthroned as the Holy One;
you are the one Israel praises.

In you our ancestors put their trust;
they trusted and you delivered them.
To you they cried out and were saved;
in you they trusted and were not put to shame.
But I am a worm and not a man,
scorned by everyone, despised by the people.
All who see me mock me;
they hurl insults, shaking their heads.
"He trusts in the LORD," they say,
"let the LORD rescue him.
Let him deliver him,
since he delights in him."
Yet you brought me out of the womb;
you made me trust in you, even at my mother's breast.
From birth I was cast on you;
from my mother's womb you have been my God.
Do not be far from me,
for trouble is near
and there is no one to help.
Many bulls surround me;
strong bulls of Bashan encircle me.
Roaring lions that tear their prey
open their mouths wide against me.
I am poured out like water,
and all my bones are out of joint.
My heart has turned to wax;
it has melted within me.
My mouth is dried up like a potsherd,
and my tongue sticks to the roof of my mouth;
you lay me in the dust of death.'

Session Focus

Both Matthew and Mark record Jesus' cry of desolation in the fifth saying from the cross: 'My God, my God, why have you forsaken me?'

Jesus is quoting Psalm 22, which sees King David facing serious troubles. David's cry of desperation is framed by incredible levels of detail, which almost perfectly describe the experience of crucifixion that Jesus was going to face. For example, David records in verses 7 and 8 a description of the mockery and insults, which includes the taunt whether God will intervene and rescue him.

This seems to mirror exactly what happened to Jesus as the crowds, the Jewish authorities, the Roman soldiers and even the criminal dying next to Him mocked Him for being 'unable' to save Himself.

David also records his own physical experience in verses 14 and 15. This acts as an uncanny description of crucifixion as bones and joints are pulled out of place, the heart is put under immense pressure, and there is a desperate sensation of thirst as the victim experiences asphyxiation as death approaches.

Finally, if you continue reading Psalm 22, David records the shame and humiliation of his experience in verses 16–18, which include the piercing of hands and feet, the contortion of the naked body to show the bones, the crowds staring and gloating, and bargaining over the victim's clothes.

Again, these descriptions match the physical experience of crucifixion where nails were driven through Jesus' hands and feet, and the crowds jeered as He died, thirsty, naked and broken. David has described Jesus' crucifixion with uncanny accuracy.

But Jesus' use of the introduction to Psalm 22 also expresses a much deeper, more agonising and more heartfelt despair at the isolation that He, God the Son, was experiencing at being alienated from God the Father. Somehow, in some profound and mysterious way, the triune God was disrupted by the cross. The consequence of Jesus carrying the crushing weight of the world's sins on His shoulders was that He and His Father were estranged. Jesus was forsaken by His Father so that we could be forgiven. He was rejected so that we could be accepted. He was estranged so that we could be adopted. He was excluded from the mercy of God so that we could be included. He was extradited so that we could be invited. Here is the ultimate act of hospitality – that Jesus would feel utterly abandoned by His Father, so that we could be rescued.

Jesus' words on the cross invite us to take a closer look at Psalm 22. This psalm not only gives us insight into what is happening at the scene – the crowds throwing their insults, the pouring out of water, the death that follows the thirst – but also into how Jesus is feeling – abandoned, desperate, alone. The emotions at the heart of His distress prove many things. They prove His humanity – He experiences pain in the same way we do. They prove His love – He went to such desperate extremes to rescue us. They prove His unique relationship with the Father – from whom He has never been separated before.

These words from the cross invite us to empathise with Jesus in His pain. But in a far more profound way, it is Jesus who is empathising with us in our pain. Because of Jesus' empathy towards us, we are invited to experience forgiveness, which we accept with deep gratitude and worship. Because of Jesus' empathy towards us, we are invited to follow His example, empathising with others in times of physical, emotional and spiritual distress.

Discussion Starters

1. When have you felt closest to God? What were the circumstances?

   _____

   _____

   _____

   _____

2. Have you ever felt abandoned by God? What were the circumstances that made you feel this way? Did you tell God how you were feeling?

   _____

   _____

   _____

   _____

3. Why do you think Jesus offered a cry of desolation from the cross?

_____
_____
_____
_____

4. How could you offer hope and comfort to someone who tells you: 'There has been so much suffering in my life I don't believe God really cares anymore'?

_____
_____
_____
_____

5. Read Psalm 22 again. What are the different elements that seem to foreshadow or predict the cross? How can we understand the cross better because of David's experiences?

_____
_____
_____
_____

6. Try to list all the ways that Jesus suffered on the cross – which ones can you relate to? How do they help you in your relationship with Him?

_____
_____
_____
_____

7. How do verses 2–3 in Psalm 22 help you trust in God, even in difficult situations?

_____
_____
_____

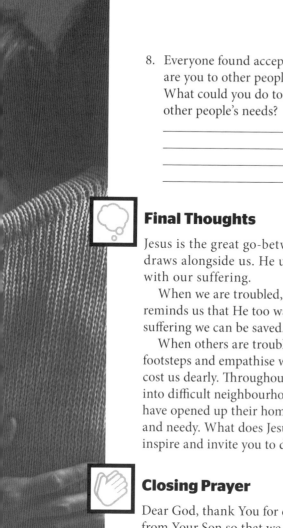

8. Everyone found acceptance from Jesus. How approachable are you to other people – especially those who are suffering? What could you do to become more empathetic towards other people's needs?

_____

_____

_____

_____

Final Thoughts

Jesus is the great go-between. He enters our world and draws alongside us. He understands us, and He identifies with our suffering.

When we are troubled, Jesus invites us to the cross where He reminds us that He too was troubled, and that because of His suffering we can be saved.

When others are troubled, Jesus invites us to follow in His footsteps and empathise with those in need even though it may cost us dearly. Throughout the ages Christians have moved into difficult neighbourhoods, or have crossed continents, or have opened up their homes to live and work among the poor and needy. What does Jesus' willingness to suffer on our behalf inspire and invite you to do?

Closing Prayer

Dear God, thank You for experiencing the pain of separation from Your Son so that we could become Your sons and daughters. Lord Jesus, thank You for enduring the cross and scorning its shame. Spirit of God, help us to empathise with those in need the way Jesus did, and to be willing to suffer that others might come to know the grace of our God. Amen.

Further Reflection

You might want to use Isaiah 53 to meditate more on Christ, the suffering servant. Books for further reading:

John Stott, *Cross of Christ* (Downers Grove, IL, USA: IVP, 1986)

N.T. Wright, *The Day the Revolution Began* (San Francisco, CA, USA: HarperOne, 2016)

Invitation to trust

'Father, into your hands I commit my spirit'

Warm Up

If you were in real trouble – perhaps financially, legally, or your life was in danger – who would you be most likely to call? What makes this person the first one you'd turn to? Who do you think would be likely to call you in similar circumstances?

Opening Prayer

Dear God, thank You that You have always been our refuge in times of trouble. Thank You for delivering us in Your righteousness. You listen to us. You are our rock and our fortress, our guide and our redeemer. Thank You for Your faithfulness. Praise You for Your mighty power. Whatever lies ahead, please help us to remember these truths, and to trust You even in our darkest moments. Amen.

Eye Opener

I remember watching an interview with a North Korean dissident and atheist. She had been sent to a brutal prison camp for her criticism of the government. Some other inmates were Christians, imprisoned because of their faith. The Christians were often singled out for torturous treatment and many died for their beliefs. The dissident explained how she had witnessed the death of some of the Christians. Watching them die with dignity despite horrific pain was the tipping point for her in coming to faith. Sometimes how we endure tragedy witnesses more eloquently to our trust in God, than how we handle prosperity.

Setting the Scene

In the last chapter we heard Jesus' cry of desolation as He experienced the crushing pain of being abandoned by His Father. How tempting it must have been at that moment to have walked away from His mission. And yet He chose to carry on. Back in the Garden of Gethsemane, Jesus had prayed to His Father to take away the cup of suffering that lay ahead. And yet, ultimately, He had submitted His will to God. As the suffering became more and more intense and the sky turned black, there was still opportunity for Jesus to pull out. With the world watching, and without disguising His pain and distress, how would Jesus end His life? As we read the Bible passages for today, look out for clues that point to this moment being mysteriously and magnificently profound.

Bible Readings

Luke 23:44–49

'It was now about noon, and darkness came over the whole land until three in the afternoon, for the sun stopped shining. And the curtain of the temple was torn in two. Jesus called out with a loud voice, "Father, into your hands I commit my spirit." When he had said this, he breathed his last. The centurion, seeing what had happened, praised God and said, "Surely this was a righteous man." When all the people who had gathered to witness this sight saw what took place, they beat their breasts and went away. But all those who knew him, including the women who had followed him from Galilee, stood at a distance, watching these things.'

Psalm 31:1–5

'In you, LORD, I have taken refuge;
let me never be put to shame;
deliver me in your righteousness.
Turn your ear to me,
come quickly to my rescue;
be my rock of refuge,
a strong fortress to save me.
Since you are my rock and my fortress,
for the sake of your name lead and guide me.
Keep me free from the trap that is set for me,
for you are my refuge.
Into your hands I commit my spirit;
deliver me, LORD, my faithful God.'

Session Focus

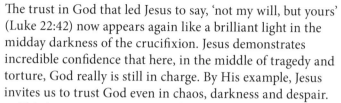

The trust in God that led Jesus to say, 'not my will, but yours' (Luke 22:42) now appears again like a brilliant light in the midday darkness of the crucifixion. Jesus demonstrates incredible confidence that here, in the middle of tragedy and torture, God really is still in charge. By His example, Jesus invites us to trust God even in chaos, darkness and despair.

This is a very important insight to hold on to. You don't have to spend long flicking through Christian television channels around the world, to find someone telling you that Jesus came to bring you happiness and health, blessings and bounty. Some even argue that if you are not experiencing riches and renown then it is due to a lack of faith on your part. But here on the cross we see the ultimate expression of faith – and yet Jesus is in agony, stripped of all His worldly goods.

The cross of Christ is a challenge to anyone who believes it is possible to follow Jesus and avoid heartache. Jesus Himself said to His disciples, 'Whoever wants to be my disciple must deny themselves and take up their cross and follow me. For whoever wants to save their life will lose it, but whoever loses their life for me and the gospel will save it. What good is it for someone to gain the whole world, yet forfeit their soul?' (Mark 8:34–37).

For 2,000 years, Christians have shown trust at the most extreme and tragic moments of their lives. Think of Stephen preaching the gospel to his executioners, and then looking up to heaven as his killers threw the stones that smashed his body. As he died, Stephen's face seemed to shine like an angel, which was to have a significant impact on one of his executioners – Saul of Tarsus, who went on to write most of our New Testament.

Consider Perpetua, a young mum who was arrested for attending a baptism class and then sentenced to death when she refused to deny her faith in Christ. In AD 203 she was put into a stadium, where she and the rest of her baptism class were attacked by wild animals, and then finally put to the sword by gladiators to the applause of the crowd. Perpetua had many opportunities to deny her faith and be released, but instead she confessed steadfast faith in God regardless, and is forever remembered for her trust in Him.

Today, men and women around the world face similar horrors. Extremist terror groups have deliberately targeted Christians in horrific acts of torture and violence, but we hear of many of these persecuted believers crying out to Jesus as they are killed. Perhaps they call out to Him because they know they have someone who really understands them; someone who has also faced executioners and remained faithful to the end, for their sake.

Jesus had a choice. At any moment He could have ended His own suffering, used the power that was His as the Son of the living God to destroy His executioners, or even the whole planet if He so wished. But His words, 'into your hands I commit my spirit' form a prayer of commitment to see His mission through to the very end. Jesus' words are taken from the beautiful Psalm 31, which is a prayer of hope and trust in God. It speaks of finding refuge in God alone – the psalmist's fortress and salvation – when times were most difficult.

The way Jesus died had an immediate and profound impact on one of His executioners – a Roman centurion. From what we know of the times, crucifixions were relatively commonplace, and yet this military officer makes a confession in light of Jesus' declaration of trust. In Mark's Gospel it is recorded that he responded: 'Surely this man was the Son of God!' (Mark 15:39). The death of Jesus may not have been a spectacular miracle like the feeding of thousands or the calming of a storm, but nevertheless, the way that Jesus died impacted this soldier and invited from his lips an acknowledgment of the presence of God.

Discussion Starters

1. Describe a time in your life when you found it very hard to trust God and a time when it was very easy.

   _____

   _____

   _____

   _____

2. There are so many stories in the Bible and throughout Christian history of women and men who have suffered or been killed for their faith. Which ones particularly inspire you?

   _____

   _____

   _____

   _____

3. At the crucifixion, God does not rescue Jesus from the agony of the cross. Why do you think God sometimes doesn't rescue people from suffering?

   _____

   _____

   _____

   _____

4. Jesus' trust in God to the bitter end helped others, beginning with the Roman Centurian, to trust God too. What in the account of the crucifixion might also help you to trust God?

   _____

   _____

   _____

   _____

5. How would you respond to someone who says: 'Christianity isn't what I expected. I don't feel anything when I worship God and I still struggle with life sometimes. Is it worth it?'

_____

_____

_____

_____

6. Read through Psalm 31:1–5. Which of the images of safety do you find most encouraging?

_____

_____

_____

_____

7. As a group, list five places globally, or people you pray for regularly, that are suffering persecution for their faith right now. Pray for them using Psalm 31:1–5 as inspiration.

_____

_____

_____

_____

8. A young Christian wants to know how to keep their faith strong, even through the tough times. How would you answer? What do you personally need to put into practice?

_____

_____

_____

_____

Final Thoughts

In Jesus' darkest moment, He entrusts Himself fully to His Father's care. There is an intimacy here as Jesus commits His spirit into His Father's hands. There is hope as Jesus knows that death is not the end. There is trust as He confidently gives His spirit into the hands which made and sustain the universe.

There is inspiration as He shows us that in the real distress of death there can also be a real assurance of God watching over us. Of God waiting to receive us. Whether we are going through times of suffering or not, none of us knows the next stage of our journey through life. Nevertheless, Jesus invites us to follow His example and commit ourselves to His God and His plans for us, fully believing and trusting in love. As Paul wrote: 'we are more than conquerors through him who loved us. For I am convinced that neither death nor life, neither angels nor demons, neither the present nor the future, nor any powers, neither height nor depth, nor anything else in all creation, will be able to separate us from the love of God that is in Christ Jesus our Lord' (Rom. 8:37–39).

Closing Prayer

Father God, into Your hands we commit our lives. We want to live every day for You. We trust You that You are our refuge, our shelter and our rock. Help us to stand with those who suffer, look out for those in need, and honour You in all circumstances. In the precious name of Jesus. Amen.

Further Reflection

You could meditate on this theme in the Bible by reading about the martyrdom of Stephen (Acts 6:5–15; 7). The following books may help you too:

Krish Kandiah, *Paradoxology: Why Christianity Was Never Meant To Be Simple* (London: Hodder & Stoughton, 2014)

Corrie ten Boom, *The Hiding Place* (Washington, CT, USA: Chosen Books, 1971)

Leader's Notes

The following notes pertain to certain discussion starters throughout this guide. They may help shed more light during your group discussions.

STUDY ONE
Invitation to forgiveness

1. The animosity of the crowd seems totally out of proportion to who Jesus is and how He has lived. Jesus' unrelenting kindness offering mercy in the face of this unremitting hatred is truly outstanding. Let's be challenged to reflect something of His magnificence into the darkness around us.

2. Jesus did not have to take the abuse He received but shows His meekness-power under control; His generosity-power for the service of others; His humility-power for their benefit. Sometimes withholding our power is the most powerful act of all.

3. You could discuss examples such as when Jesus used a whip to drive marketeers from the Temple, when He argued back with the devil in the wilderness, and when He told stories to stump the critical Pharisees. Jesus was not afraid to speak unpopular truths.

4. It would be worth reminding the group that forgiveness does not imply that the sin or crime committed is inconsequential. Quite the opposite. God takes sin so seriously that He doesn't just dismiss it. Jesus dies in order that sin can be forgiven; a punishment is meted; a price is paid.

5. We can sometimes excuse our anger and lack of forgiveness because of how we are feeling, or our circumstances. Jesus' forgiveness under extreme circumstances models godly forgiveness.

7. This could be discussed in the context of individuals' experience of the invitation to receive forgiveness from Jesus.

8. Encourage your group to be honest here. Perhaps if you, the leader, set an example of an area you are struggling with, it will unlock openness in your group.

STUDY TWO
Invitation to service

1. Jesus demonstrates that the life of faith embraces not just the 'spiritual' or ceremonial parts, but all parts of our lives, the practical and the physical too. Food also brings people together and Jesus is continually seeking to do that, bringing enemies together around a shared table. He explains His own identity as the bread of life and the bringer of living water, and our future in terms of a heavenly banquet.

2. Jesus' need for food and drink demonstrates that He really is human. But it also shows a humility that He is willing to let someone else meet His needs. Jesus really is the omnipotent God, yet He invites us to serve Him, and empowers us by His willingness to be reliant on us.

3. Jesus identifies with sinful humanity through His baptism, death and resurrection, but He particularly identifies with the poor and needy. If we love Jesus and seek to follow Him, we will naturally live out His affection for those most in need.

4. Jesus cared for the sick, the hungry and the needy, and He also preached the gospel. To separate out practical and spiritual help is to separate what the Bible locks firmly together.

5. You could discuss here the parable of the good Samaritan, the woman at the well, the feeding of the 5,000 Jesus' mission statement from Isaiah that He quotes in Luke 4:18, His instructions on who to include at a dinner party in Luke 14, the parable of the great banquet.

6. As a leader, make sure you are prepared with practical ways that your church is responding to needs in your community, and ways for people to follow up on this study with practical service.

8. It reminds us of the one who is the water of life, who went thirsty on the cross in order to make sure we stand right before God. The one who poured out His blood for us. The one we remember during Holy Communion. It reminds us to hunger and thirst after righteousness, to look out for others who are thirsty around us, and that we have a spiritual thirst that can only be satisfied in a relationship with Jesus.

STUDY THREE
Invitation to hope

1. How can a man dying next to Jesus not realise he is in the presence of God, and use his last few words to sneer at Jesus rather than ask for help – especially when the other criminal could so clearly grasp who He was and what He was doing? This other criminal could see what the learned religious leaders and even Jesus' own disciples failed to see. It is also strange perhaps that Jesus does not ask the criminal to repent, publicly or privately, of his sins first. There is no baptism; there are no good deeds.

2. These are very encouraging words from Jesus to a dying man, but let's not forget that he still had to face a horribly painful death. However, he could have known something of the peace and assurance that comes not from feelings, but from the fact of Jesus' words.

65

4. For the thief on the cross, it was Jesus' words that were the foundation of his hope. Knowing our Bibles and recognising their contents as God's words to us can be the foundation of our hope too. Another way for our confidence to grow comes in seeing God prove faithful in our lives as we trust and obey Him.

5. Encourage people to chat in pairs to make it easier for them to share in the wider group.

6. For many believers the main challenges for sharing faith are: embarrassment, lack of confidence, bad experiences sharing faith in the past, not knowing what to say, risking ruining a relationship, scaring people away from faith, not seeing the opportunities, not feeling that sharing faith is appropriate in this culture. Give people room to be honest. Ask them how these hurdles can be overcome.

STUDY FOUR
Invitation to adoption

1. It's not just our relationship with God that Jesus sorts out on the cross. His care and attention to His mother here shows us that in death as in life, Jesus is also reconciling people with each other. Even as He bears the weight of the sins of the world, He is caring for the people in need in front of Him. His overarching mission does not prevent Him from looking out for the needs of His own mother.

2. Galatians 4:1–7 is very clear that our redemption is a preparation for our adoption into God's family. By making sure His own mother is 'adopted', Jesus gives a hint of this in the crucifixion scene itself. But there is also a demonstration that at the heart of the Christian faith is the message of adoption and forgiveness, not only effective when we die, but right now.

3. Jesus had every excuse here to focus on His mission – to die for the sins of the world. But He chooses to be 'other-centred'. Even in the midst of the crisis and agony of the cross, He cares for His family and friends.

4. We may often think of worship as the quality of our music or the preaching when we gather for church services. This is not how worship is defined in the Bible. The cross of Christ shows us that Christianity is about taking action on behalf of those in need. Perhaps it is because God Himself cares so deeply for people in need, that He wants to see that heartbeat evidenced in our lives too.

5. In the ancient world there was no welfare state and, because of the patriarchal society, adult men were often the bread winners in a household. With 5,000 children in need of adoption in the UK (over 100,000 in the USA) and in the region of 9,000 more foster carers needed, there are plenty of opportunities for Christians to demonstrate care for the orphan. See www.homeforgood.org.uk for more information.

7. If the measure of our worship to God is our care for the widow and the orphan and yet there are still 5,000 children waiting in care to be adopted, perhaps we need to reclaim our theology of adoption so we understand better what God has done for us. Perhaps we could reclaim our responsibility as God's people to take the lead in looking out for the most vulnerable in our society.

8. Let's be active both in evangelism – the invitation to others to be welcomed into the family of God, and in hospitality – the invitation to others to be welcomed into our homes. This may be an invitation to the elderly, singles, students, children in care, ex-offenders etc. Think through the areas where your church may be best placed to serve.

STUDY FIVE
Invitation to empathy

3. Jesus knew what was going to happen to Him – He had predicted it all through His life, but there was still an element of shock as He was wrenched from His Father. In the Garden of Gethsemane, Jesus is so stressed by what is about to happen to Him that He sweats blood and talks of being 'overwhelmed with sorrow to the point of death' (Matt. 26:38). So, for there to be genuine despair at the reality of the cross is not out of the question.

4. Jesus can sympathise with this as He was 'a man of suffering, and familiar with pain' (Isa. 53:3). By citing Psalm 22 Jesus shows the extent of His pain and agony, yet He also hints at His ongoing faith in God – see Psalm 22:22 onwards.

6. Jesus suffered physical agony, social ostracism, verbal abuse, spiritual alienation and legal injustice. Take time to listen to one another, as these sorts of sufferings are common.

8. Growing in our capacity for hospitality towards others can start as simply as bringing a cake to work, offering help to our neighbours, or promising to pray for a colleague. Praying for opportunities to see the needs of others and finding a way to help might just change your life.

STUDY SIX
Invitation to trust

1. Set the example by being open about something in your own life.

3. It is hard for us to hear, but the cross shows us that sometimes God has a higher purpose than our immediate alleviation of pain. God the Father loves Jesus the Son fully and perfectly, and yet He still didn't rescue Him because His pain was achieving something of infinite worth.

Sometimes God will allow us to experience pain and suffering to achieve another goal that we may only come to realise when we see it from the perspective of eternity.

4. We see the fulfilment of prophecy in Psalm 22. Jesus enduring the cross for us convinces us of the depth of love He has for us. God the Father allowing Jesus to endure all of this for us, again underlines God's commitment to us.

5. Jesus does not give us an example of a perfect, happy, fulfilled life, with no pain or anguish or difficulties, nor does He promise us this sort of life while we are on earth. We are told there is a cost to becoming a Christian, but it's nothing compared to eternal life and relationship with the creator, and forgiveness and adoption into His family. We can also be assured that whatever happens, God will be standing right alongside us.

7. If you cannot think of places around the world where it is hard to be a Christian, then pray for Christians in North Korea, Eritrea, Iraq, South Sudan, Pakistan and Syria. Perhaps visit www.opendoorsuk.org for the latest information on how to pray for the Persecuted Church.

EASTER

WHAT HAPPENS NEXT?

40 Days with Jesus is a post-Easter resource for individuals, small groups and churches. At its heart it is an invitation to actively explore the accounts of the risen Jesus and the impact He had on those He encountered.

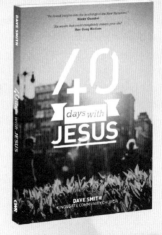

Written by Dave Smith
ISBN: 978-1-78259-138-2
Bulk order discounts available for churches and small groups.

 Also available in eBook formats

01 For you:
A 40-day devotional underpinning the whole series

02 For your small group:
Free video teaching and small group studies

03 For your church:
Free sermon outlines

To find out how you can get involved, visit **40days.info**

SmallGroup central

All of our small group ideas and resources in one place

Online:

smallgroupcentral.org.uk
is filled with free video teaching, tools, articles and a whole host of ideas.

On the road:

A range of seminars themed for small groups can be brought to your local community. Contact us at
hello@smallgroupcentral.org.uk

In print:

Books, study guides and DVDs covering an extensive list of themes, Bible books and life issues.

Find out more at:
smallgroupcentral.org.uk

Courses and events

Waverley Abbey College

Publishing and media

Conference facilities

Transforming lives

CWR's vision is to enable people to experience personal transformation through applying God's Word to their lives and relationships.

Our Bible-based training and resources help people around the world to:
• Grow in their walk with God
• Understand and apply Scripture to their lives
• Resource themselves and their church
• Develop pastoral care and counselling skills
• Train for leadership
• Strengthen relationships, marriage and family life and much more.

Our insightful writers provide daily Bible reading notes and other resources for all ages, and our experienced course designers and presenters have gained an international reputation for excellence and effectiveness.

CWR's Training and Conference Centre in Surrey, England, provides excellent facilities in an idyllic setting – ideal for both learning and spiritual refreshment.

CWR Applying God's Word
to everyday life and relationships

CWR, Waverley Abbey House,
Waverley Lane, Farnham,
Surrey GU9 8EP, UK

Telephone: **+44 (0)1252 784700**
Email: **info@cwr.org.uk**
Website: **cwr.org.uk**

Registered Charity No. 294387
Company Registration No. 1990308